SARATOGA

The Ultimate Racing Experience

SARATOGA

The Ultimate Racing Experience

Text by

Frank R. Scatoni

Photos by

Horsephotos

DRF PRESS

Published by
Daily Racing Form Press
100 Broadway, 7th Floor
New York, NY 10005

ISBN: 0-9726401-6-9
Library of Congress Control Number: 2003113623

Jacket designed by Chris Donofry
Text design by Pauline Neuwirth, Neuwirth and Associates, Inc.

Printed in China

Contents

Marylou Whitney with trainer Nick Zito.

FOREWORD

BY MARYLOU WHITNEY

I hope heaven is as beautiful as Saratoga Springs in August!

I FIRST LAID EYES on the Spa City in the fall of 1958. My husband, Cornelius "Sonny" Vanderbilt Whitney, had brought me to finalize the sale of his summer home, Cady Hill House. After spending only one day in this enchanting town, I decided we could not abandon it. Although over the years Saratoga had become a bit run-down and devoid of people, the town smiled at me! I learned right away that there was no other community in the world that embraced its residents like Saratoga Springs. I loved the feel of Saratoga so much I offered to buy the property from my husband. He told me that if I loved the house and town so much, it must have great potential. Forty-five years later, Saratoga is not only "the Summer Place to Be," it is my main home.

As America's oldest arena for Thoroughbred racing, Saratoga Springs has always had the best racing in the country. However, very few people were coming to the track back in the 1950s. Sonny told me how his grandfather, William C. Whitney, with the help of a couple of investors, purchased the track to save it from almost certain demolition in the early 1900s. Sonny was very discouraged at how Saratoga Race Course seemed to be again following the same path. He asked me if I had any ideas on how we might help restore this region to its former glory. I read every history book I could find on the Spa City. I fell in love with the Victorian opulence of the days of "Diamond Jim" Brady, and I set out to restore those grand times.

The people who have been charged with running and promoting our Saratoga racetrack have preserved the old feel and elegance of days gone by. Their wisdom has allowed for growth and demand, while still maintaining tradition. Walking into the grandstand still makes me feel as though I just stepped back into the racing world of the 19th century. There is no other track in America that has the ambiance and charm of Saratoga. World-class racing could have no finer setting than my beloved Saratoga Springs.

Saratoga: The Ultimate Racing Experience showcases Saratoga at its best. Future generations will look to this book as an illustration of the grand times in the 21st century. Reading about Saratoga's past is wonderful. However, living in Saratoga Springs today is even better.

"For such as pass this testing faithfully, there is a reward appointed. It is a green and pleasant heaven, shaded by lofty elms. It has a lake and canna lilies and swans and a stately fountain and time—and sometimes cool winds bellying down from the Adirondacks. The customers can say to each other, 'Well, we behaved at Jamaica, and sure enough, here we are at Saratoga.'"

—JOE H. PALMER, "Saratoga, or the Horse at Home"

INTRODUCTION

The August Place to Be

"Gone now are the old hotels, the gambling houses, even the tracks by which trainloads of the nation's wealthy and great, beauty and sport were brought for a hundred Augusts to the platform in the Grand Union courtyard with their Saratoga Trunks.

"All things change, Saratoga perhaps more slowly than most . . . Unchanged, however, is the place to be in August."

—Kent Hollingsworth, *The Archjockey of Canterbury and Other Tales*

For almost a century and a half, Saratoga Race Course in Saratoga Springs, New York, has been the August place to be for Thoroughbred racing. And while things change slowly in Saratoga, as Kent Hollingsworth noted above, the recent addition of racing dates in July and September now makes Saratoga "the summer place to be." Equine greats such as Man o' War, Whirlaway, Secretariat, Seattle Slew, Affirmed, Alydar, and Ruffian, and more recent favorites such as Go For Wand and Point Given, have all graced this historic track. Legendary trainers and jockeys such as "Sunny Jim" Fitzsimmons and Eddie Arcaro, Woody Stephens and Angel Cordero, D. Wayne Lukas and Jerry Bailey, have all made Saratoga their August home. And each year, hundreds of thousands of race fans, vacationers, and artists have turned this rustic, idyllic upstate New York town into a festive and exciting place—and it's all because of Thoroughbred racing.

For the 2003 race meet, Harold Roth and his Horsephotos team scoured the track from the earliest light, capturing everything from the behind-the-scenes preparations on the backstretch to paddock parades and celebrations in the winners' circle, bringing Saratoga to life in vivid, vibrant photographs. The result is *Saratoga: The Ultimate Racing Experience*, a collection of photos that captures the essence of the Saratoga race meet and presents an unprecedented look at the town, the track, and the Thoroughbreds that make Saratoga one of the most visited venues in the history of the sport.

The book opens with an overview of the racetrack—the paddock, the clubhouse, the silks room, and the infield and its great lake—and then the trip begins in earnest, in the morning, where the Thoroughbreds gather on the track for their daily workouts. As the August sun cuts through the misty haze of the cool Adirondack air, backstretch workers tend to the horses while sharp-eyed trainers study their runners' every move.

The photos then take us through race day: from the paddock to the track, from the post parade to the starting gate, from the finish line to the winners' circle. In between, the reader will get glimpses of life at Saratoga, images of what makes this track and meet so special: the pomp and circumstance of the private clubhouse boxes, the punters in the grandstand, the picnickers out back, the horses rushing from the starting gate, and the bird's-eye view from the race caller's perch high above the track.

Along the way, we visit people—jockeys, trainers, exercise riders, grooms, and even the track bugler—as well as places: the barns, the backstretch, and Fasig-Tipton's Humphrey S. Finney Pavilion, the site of that company's yearling sales as well as the Hall of Fame induction ceremony. We also weave through town, straight up Broadway, pausing for stops at Congress Park and the Adelphi Hotel, and then snaking off to Siro's, Yaddo, the Saratoga Performing Arts Center, and the Hall of Springs.

As you'll see, the 2003 meet was a special one. Funny Cide fever hit the track like an epidemic, and though the New York-bred gelding who had captured the first two legs of the Triple Crown earlier in the year failed to race at his upstate owners' home track, his fans came out in droves, sporting Funny Cide T-shirts and hats, playing with Funny Cide bobbleheads, and sipping Funny Cide beer from Funny Cide cups. Ten Most Wanted, ridden by lifetime-earnings record holder Pat Day, captured the 134th running of the Travers, and Silver Wagon upset a bunch of hopefuls in the Hopeful. Most impressive, however, were the performances of trainer Todd Pletcher and jockey John Velazquez, who set new records for win totals on the meet. Together the duo teamed up for 29 wins, with Pletcher taking home the training title with 35 victories, and Velazquez capturing the riding title with 61.

On the track business was booming. The meet set single-day records for attendance and handle and the record for overall attendance—all this despite the weather: The first half of the meet was swamped by torrential rains.

But Saratoga prevailed over the weather—as it always has prevailed throughout its long and storied history. It witnessed the end of the Civil War and lived through two World Wars, with World War II temporarily halting racing; it also persevered through the Hughes anti-gambling law, which curtailed racing from 1911 through 1913. Other than those two interruptions, live racing has taken place at Saratoga every year since 1863, making it one of the oldest racetracks in America, and making its signature race, the Travers, the oldest stakes race for 3-year-olds in America.

Saratoga's first meet was held on August 3, 1863, when thousands of tourists and locals took time out from sampling the curative powers of the various Saratoga springs and helped kick off the inaugural summer meeting at what is now referred to as Horse Haven. An advertisement in the *Daily Saratogian* screamed RUNNING RACES! AT SARATOGA . . . TWO RACES EACH DAY! And though the first race ever run was only a two-horse affair, it was won by a 3-year-old filly named Lizzie W., who soundly defeated a highly touted 3-year-old colt named Captain Moore, in a best-of-three series of races.

It was an auspicious start to an auspicious meeting, and though the Saratoga Association, headed by William Travers, would build a new, permanent racecourse on today's current site the following year, from that first day forward, Saratoga would live up to its eventual nickname, the Graveyard of Favorites. Over the next 100-plus years, some of the greatest horses in the history of the sport were beaten at this historic track. Man o' War was upset by Upset, of course; Triple Crown winner Gallant Fox fell to 100-1 shot Jim Dandy; Onion fouled up Secretariat's Whitney; New York Filly Triple Crown winner Davona Dale was outfooted by It's in the Air; and in 1982, the winner of each Triple Crown race—Gato Del Sol, Aloma's Ruler, and Conquistador Cielo—suffered defeat at the feet of Runaway Groom in the Travers.

The track, however, has also been the site of some incredible performances by incredible horses. Exterminator won the 1 3/4-mile Saratoga Cup three times before "Old Bones" retired at age nine; Discovery won three consecutive Whitneys; Native Dancer swept four major juvenile races in 1952; Jaipur and Ridan dueled in one of the most thrilling Travers renewals ever; Affirmed and Alydar clashed in one of the most controversial runnings of the Travers; in 1993, Sea Hero became the first Kentucky Derby winner in 51 years to also win the Travers; and Saratoga regular Fourstardave proved his incredible longevity by winning a race in eight straight Saratoga seasons.

And the triumphs haven't been all equine, either. Angel Cordero won 11 straight riding titles and 13 in 14 years; Jerry Bailey had two consecutive years with 50-plus wins; and John Velazquez won six races in one day.

Perhaps this is what made the 2003 meet so special: Amid all that history, all that triumph, Todd Pletcher and John Velazquez rewrote the record books. But their achievements came as no great surprise. In a town that makes its name by trading in mineral springs and Thoroughbreds, extraordinary things are bound to happen. And that's what makes Saratoga so special—it's a place full of miracles. You have to see it to believe it, and this collection of photographs from the 2003 season helps bring those miracles to life.

The first word of this sign says it all: historic.

CHAPTER ONE

THE TRACK

"I rather think that the charm of Saratoga is that it represents, to those to whom racing is a way of life, something to which they may need return. It is, of course, the oldest track in America, and its ways are old-fashioned ways. After eleven months of new-fashioned ways, it is as restful as old slippers, as quiet as real joy."

—JOE H. PALMER, "Saratoga, or the Horse at Home"

IN JOE PALMER'S terrific newspaper story "Saratoga, or the Horse at Home," he relates the tale of a Floridian horseplayer who couldn't imagine that Saratoga was possibly all that it cracked up to be—naturally, this fellow thought it was a typical New York myth perpetuated by those from the big city, especially Palmer, who had written so fondly of the town and the track in many of his columns. "The visitor," Palmer wrote, "was a quite estimable character with a gibing tongue, who disapproved of the elms because

they had no coconuts on them." So, instead of taking the newspaperman's words at face value, the visitor got up early and had a look for himself. He had to see why Palmer, a rather cynical newspaper veteran, had such a soft spot for the Spa.

A panoramic view of Saratoga Race Course.

They're not the twin spires of Churchill Downs, but Saratoga's unmistakable spires loom boldly on the horizon.

"After a treatment which included such items as being fed blueberries on the clubhouse porch, inspecting the new puppies at Max Hirsch's stable, and listening to Bob Robertson tell four stories, parts of which may possibly have been true," Palmer wrote, "he gathered himself for an estimate. It was plain he didn't like what he had to do.

"'All right,' he said, 'you win. I see it.'"

And this man had yet to go to the races!

Palmer ended his tale in typical, biting fashion, with the following line: "The firing squad was signaled to disperse."

That's the kind of loyalty that Saratoga engenders.

So what is it that makes Saratoga Race Course so special? That's a question that draws a different answer from everyone. For some, it's the quality of the racing; for others, it's the down-home feel of the track. Some folks can't resist picnicking out back, under the shade of the giant elms; others enjoy the elegance of the box seats and the clubhouse. The most telling thing, however, is that the racetrack has something for everybody.

The first race was held at Saratoga on August 3, 1863, just one month after the Battle of Gettysburg came to an end. The images in this chapter show just some of the things that make Saratoga Race Course such a treasure. It's steeped in history, but it also represents the future. After all, racing is reliant on meets like Saratoga—for it is here that old fans make their summer home and new fans get hooked on the sport.

The symbol of New York racing.

To get into the track, you must first run the gauntlet of tip-sheet touts, including these two colorful shills for

the "Pink Sheet," which features The Saratogian's *daily selections. Once inside, you can spend your money more wisely: buying a rose.*

SEA HERO
ROKEBY STABLES, UPPERVILLE, VIRGINIA
CHAMPAGNE STAKES, 1992 · KENTUCKY DERBY, 1993
THE TRAVERS, 1993

Saratoga's paddock is one of the nicest in all of racing. Smack dab in the middle of it stands this statue of 1993 Kentucky Derby winner Sea Hero, who also won that year's Travers.

The saddling area of the paddock—though some trainers choose to saddle their horses under the giant elms that tower over the walking ring.

The fans came in droves to see local hero Funny Cide, out for an afternoon stroll around the paddock.

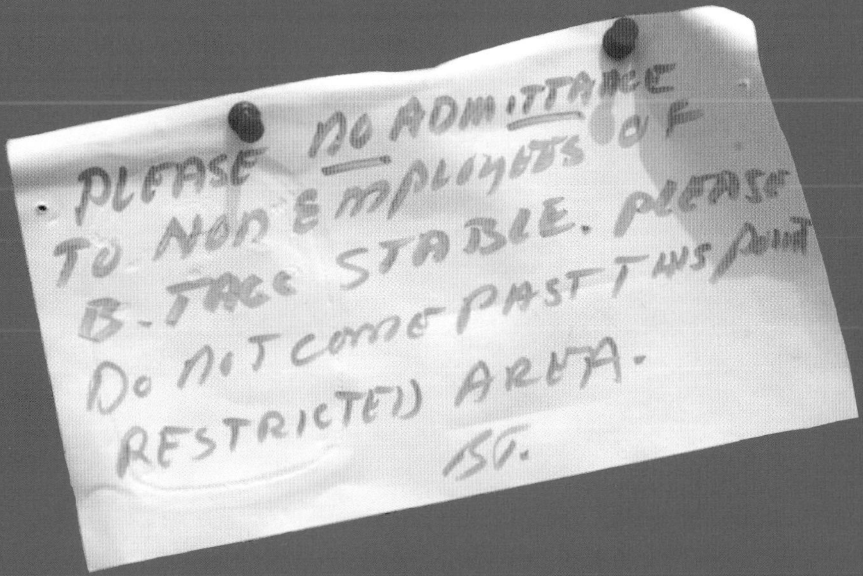

It would take more than this sign to keep fans and curiosity seekers away from Barclay Tagg's stable area—the summer home of Funny Cide.

The colors of the rainbow—and plenty more.

The jockeys' silks (left) *and the horses' saddlecloths are ready for race day.*

The familiar red-and-white signage of the racetrack, instructing the horsemen about the morning's activities.

Some things never change, even with the advent of new technology: the "Changes/Scratch" sign that adorns the track's infield.

The tombstone commemorating the career of Go For Wand, which included Spa victories in the Test and the Alabama. The champion filly broke down during the 1990 Breeders' Cup Distaff at Belmont Park and was buried at Saratoga the next day.

A subtle reminder that Sir Barton captured the 1919 Triple Crown. Other placards honor the sport's 11 Triple Crown winners.

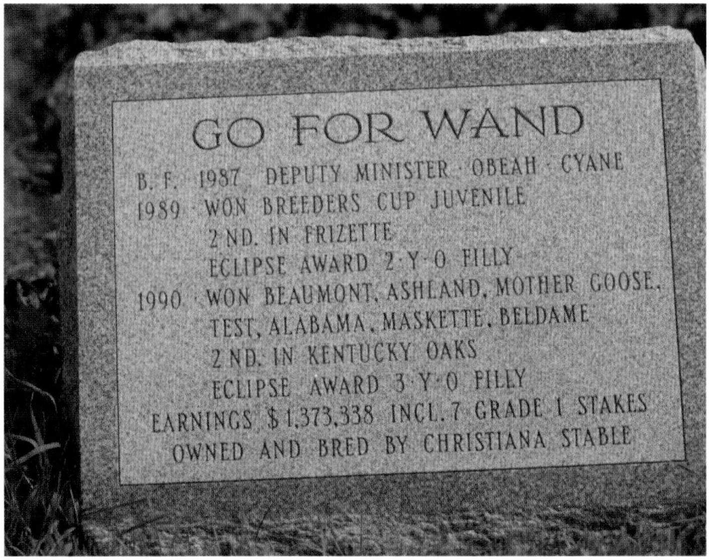

This sign is a fitting reminder that Hall of Famer Julie Krone and champion steeplechase jockey Blythe Miller have had memorable achievements at Saratoga.

Saratoga has long been the inspiration for writers and artists alike, and you can always find a painter or two rendering an image of the track.

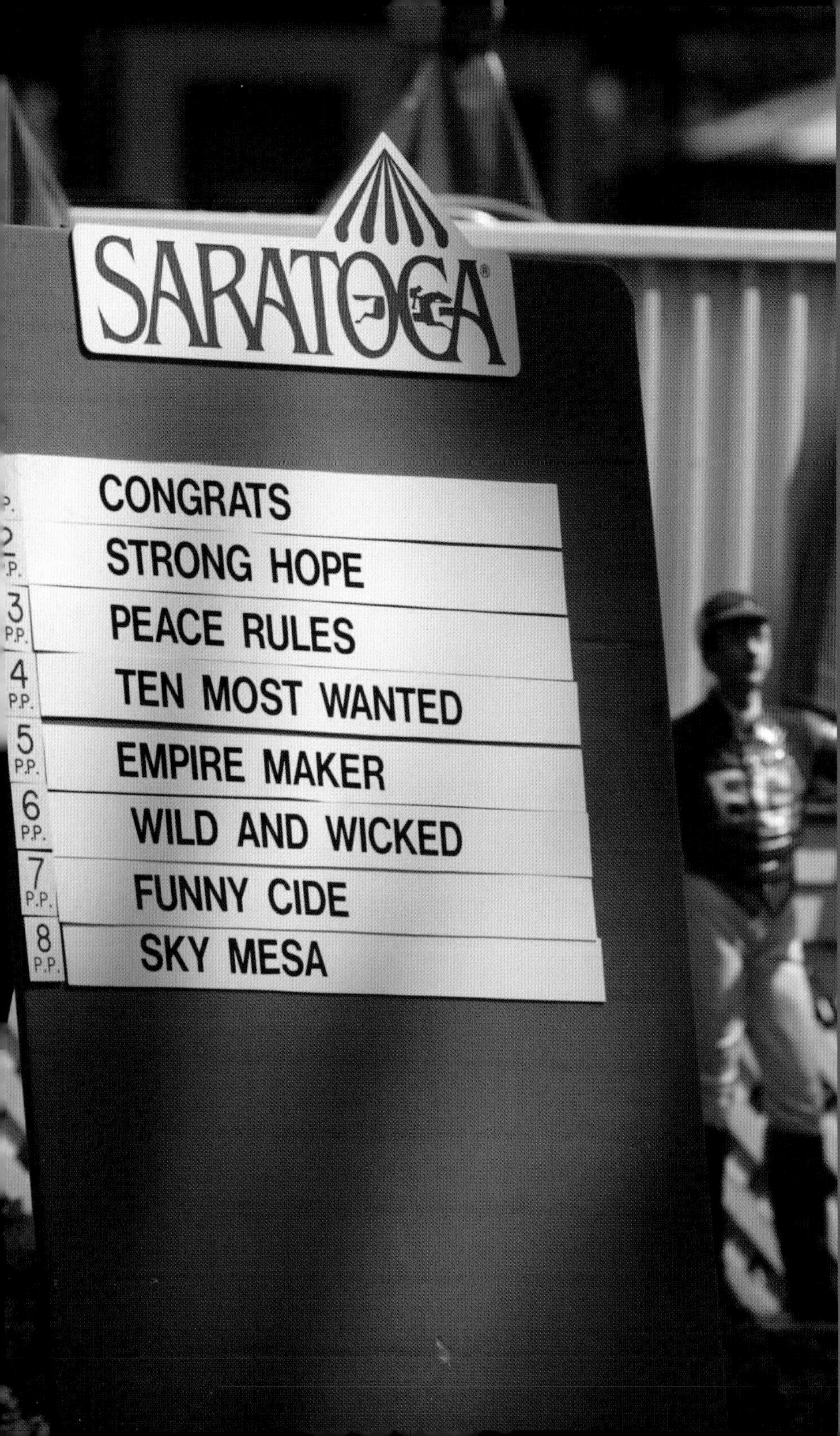

The Travers draw gets posted in the paddock, next to the defending champ's lawn jockey—in this case, 2002 Travers winner Medaglia d'Oro. Unfortunately, horses 5 and 7 were later scratched from the big race.

The changing of the guard: Medaglia d'Oro's silks get replaced by those of Travers winner Ten Most Wanted on both the lawn jockey and the canoe.

"There is, in the Saratoga infield, a lake. On this floats, and has floated since 1620, a small blue canoe. For some years I have tried to find out why it is there, though being lazy naturally and by personal inclination as well, I have not been very persistent about it. Ask one of the older veterans of Saratoga and he smiles mysteriously and shakes his head silently. This is intended to mean he isn't telling. Actually it means he doesn't know."

—Joe H. Palmer,
"Saratoga, or the Horse at Home"

A view from the clubhouse—down the escalator that leads from the clubhouse to the track's backyard area, where racegoers can eat, drink, and be very merry, particularly if they're having a winning day.

The press box at Saratoga is legendary, and the New York Racing Association is dedicated to keeping it that way. All of the great chroniclers of the sport—from Joe Palmer and Red Smith to Joe Hirsch and Steven Crist—have passed through the Saratoga press box.

You can always buy a copy of the Daily Racing Form, *naturally, but did you know that you could also buy stamps?*

There is a big pot of gold

at the end of this rainbow.

CHAPTER TWO

Saratoga Sunrise

"But for persons of less avid experience, I give you Saratoga at the third set, or the second-cup-of-coffee stage when you can begin to see a little, out of one eye. Breakfast on the clubhouse porch is particularly recommended, if only for that sublime sense of sitting at ease and watching other people work."

—Joe H. Palmer, "Saratoga, or the Horse at Home"

IMAGINE THIS: a brisk August morning; a gathering of cumulus clouds dots the blue-and-gold sky; a brilliant sun peers over the horizon. From the mist, the thundering sounds of hooves break the silence. The sun's ascent continues in the northern sky, finally illuminating the glory and grandeur that is Saratoga Race Course. Horses work, jockeys silently count the cadence of a runner's stride, trainers look diligently after their charges, grooms groom, hotwalkers walk, and thousands of fans gather in anticipation for the day's events.

Saratoga mornings are one of a kind—or as the famed horse trader Humphrey S. Finney once put it, "Mornings at Saratoga are the best that nature has to offer." He was right. Mornings at Saratoga soothe the soul, and time stands still. It's something to watch the horses move; some prancing and galloping, others blazing through furious fractions—but all snorting and frolicking and enjoying the crisp Saratoga air.

The trainers, jockeys, and backstretch workers rise early to get the first set of horses out . . . and the sun also rises.

Morning breaks as the sun peeks through the clouds in the summer sky.

This is a sublime experience for the racing fan. You can get a king's breakfast in the clubhouse; you can sit in the stands and listen to Mary Ryan's voice echoing the play-by-play of the workouts, as you sip your coffee and scour your *Daily Racing Form* for the day's winners; or you can tour the backstretch, checking out the barns where great horses once summered and new challengers wait to make their mark. The workers who care for and feed the horses are up at the crack of dawn to make sure the cheapest claimer is tended to with the same care they would give Secretariat. The dedication of these men and women is palpable. It's all about the horse. Never in your life will you see so many folks smiling at six o'clock in the morning—the workers and the fans—with the joy of being around horses.

The images in this chapter re-create a robust Saratoga morning. All of the action is there—from the workouts on the main track and the Oklahoma training track to the business on the backside. To experience a Saratoga morning is to experience the racetrack as it is, day to day, before the fanfare of the races. It's the track and the fans and the workers stripped to their barest essence. It is the purest view of the sport—and of a life around horses.

"At Saratoga, the mornings are almost as much a part of the show as the afternoons, and since some of the stable area is as open to view as the Pennsylvania Station, a visitor doesn't have to know a man or have a badge to get a pretty fair idea of the entire show."

—Joe H. Palmer, "Saratoga, or the Horse at Home"

Exercise riders greet the day and each other . . .

. . . and get to work.

The main track

bustles with action,

as trainers and

owners look on.

A groom watches the action of a horse on the Oklahoma training track.

On the backside, grooms and hotwalkers tend to their charges . . .

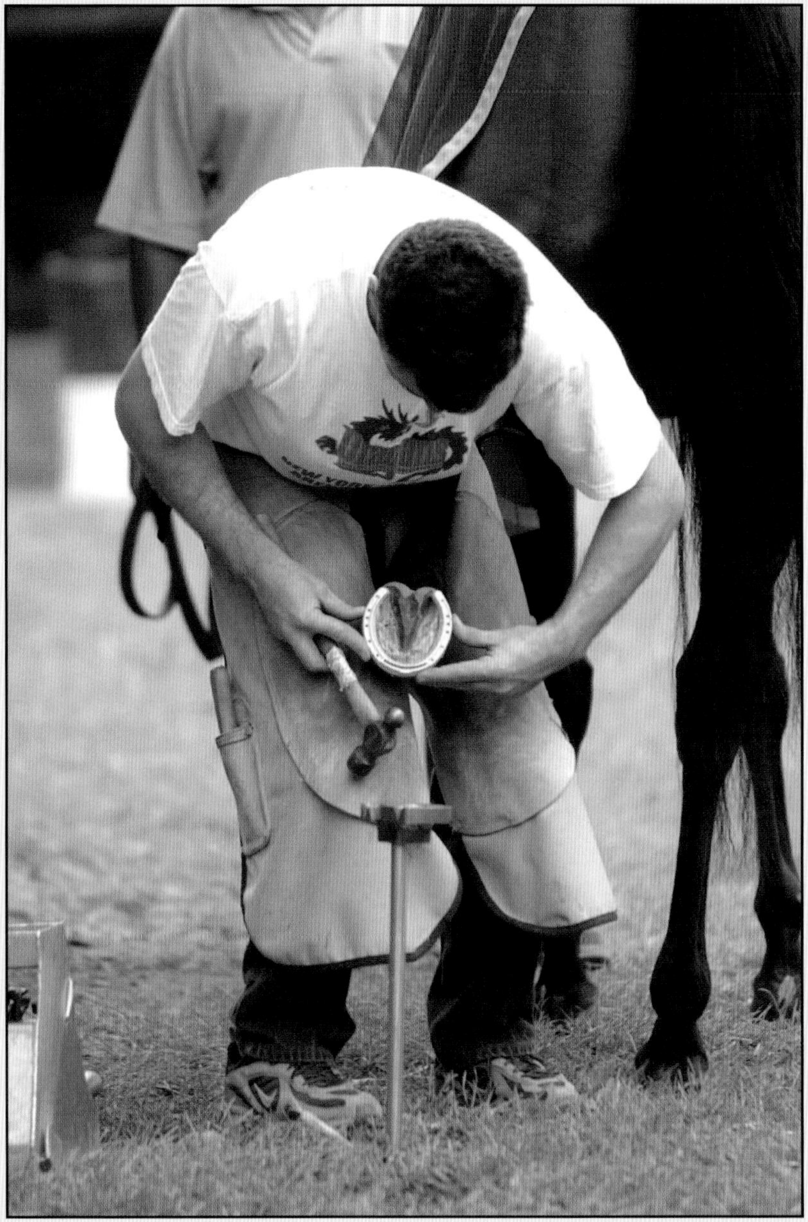

. . . while farriers make sure the horses' hooves are properly shod.

There's more to do in the morning than just watch horses work out: Start off with a backside tour, top it off with breakfast in the clubhouse, then watch Mary Ryan conduct her live TV interview before the races.

Mornings at Saratoga are the best that nature has to offer. If there is anything better than having melon, scrambled eggs, and coffee on the clubhouse porch while watching horses work, I haven't found it.

—Humphrey S. Finney, *Fair Exchange*

Trainer Nick Zito relays instructions to his exercise rider.

Jockey Aaron Gryder and trainer Ken McPeek exchange information.

Take Charge Lady takes charge during her workout.

With Anticipation (upper left), *Saarland* (lower left),

and Sky Mesa tend to their business.

Cooling off after a workout.

Local hero Funny Cide (far right), *looking regal in stall number 5 of Barclay Tagg's barn.*

5
FUNNY CIDE

Peace Rules checks out the rest of Bobby Frankel's barn, while Empire Maker buries his face in a feed tub.

"No other track draws so many non-working people in the mornings, and some of the trainers don't like it because their owners come out and see what they're doing."

—Joe H. Palmer,
"Saratoga, or the Horse at Home"

No one said that working horses was easy work.

Just another day in paradise.

6

CHAPTER THREE

A Day at the Races

"For the casual racegoer, Saratoga is about the only place in the East where he can see racing. Elsewhere he merely sees the races, which isn't the same thing at all."

—Joe H. Palmer, "Saratoga, or the Horse at Home"

"And they're off!"

THOSE THREE WORDS are music to a racing fan's ears. Nine, ten, sometimes twelve times a day at Saratoga, a racing fan gets to experience the thrill that comes with the start of a horse race. For six weeks out of the year, Saratoga Race Course is the site of the best racing in America. Bar none. The names of stakes races read like a history of the sport: the Whitney, Travers, Go For Wand, Alabama, Alfred G. Vanderbilt, Hopeful, Fourstardave . . . and the list goes on. Racing at Saratoga is a fan's delight.

The track has been the site of some of the most epic battles—heroic victories and improbable defeats—in the history of the sport. The mighty Man o' War and the superb Secretariat fell to Upset and Onion, respectively. The South reversed the Civil War defeat when Harry Bassett defeated the Northern-based Longfellow. Jaipur and Ridan dueled head and head around the track in one of the most thrilling races ever. Alydar and Affirmed renewed their legendary rivalry in the 1978 Travers, this time with Alydar coming out ahead via disqualification. And in 2001, Point Given rolled to immortality when his Travers victory made him the first horse in history to win four million-dollar-plus races in a row (with victories also in the Preakness, Belmont, and Haskell). Great horses exhibit great talent at great venues, and Saratoga has been a part of that over its many years.

Medaglia d'Oro guts it out in the Whitney.

The photos in this chapter take the viewer through a day at the races—from the paddock to the post parade, from the starting gate to the winners' circle, and everywhere in between. If you've been to Saratoga, then you already know what it is to experience a full day of racing there—it's like nothing else the sport has to offer. If you're new to the Spa experience, then these images will put you right in the thick of the action as the horses charge into the first turn, or the steeplechasers sail over the last fence, or the bettors root their winners home, or the picnickers enjoy just another day in the shade of the backyard elms. When Sam the bugler belts out the "Call to the Post," everyone knows what it means: The next race is only 10 minutes away.

Strong Hope fends off Empire Maker in the Jim Dandy.

A familiar sight every day of the week except Tuesday, the "dark day": the track's main entrance on Union Avenue.

Once inside, some racing fans pack the apron for a glimpse of the horses, while others enjoy a leisurely lunch.

The previous year's Grade 1 stakes winners greet racegoers at the clubhouse entrance to the track.

> For four weeks in August, Saratoga becomes the town of 'Health, History, and Horses'—a place of pilgrimage, thronging with believers, swells, and touts who come to revive their spirits and renew their faith in racing.
>
> —Carol Flake, *Tarnished Crown*

Handicappers study the Daily Racing Form, *looking for the day's winners.*

Whether it's on the dirt, on the turf, or over the jumps, the racing at Saratoga is the best in the country for six weeks out of the year.

1

The horses are saddled under the giant elms of the paddock, then paraded around the walking ring for all to see.

Four tractors prep the track for the next race.

At 17 minutes to post, the famous Saratoga bell clangs; then, at 10 minutes to post, Sam the bugler plays the "Call to the Post," and the horses make their way out to the track.

"The horses are on the track . . ."

"They're in the gate . . ."

". . . and they're off!"

SAL

Race caller Tom Durkin surveys the course from his perch high above the track . . .

. . . and owners maintain their focus as the horses enter the homestretch.

The crowd flocks to the rail

for the stretch run.

10

The judges scrutinize the running of the race.

Medaglia d'Oro, with the white star, finishes strongly in the Whitney; jockey Jerry Bailey celebrates in the winners' circle.

Anything can happen during the races: Here, a loose horse leads the field.

The steeplechasers get ready for a walk-up start (left); *once the action is under way, it's all thrills until the last horse crosses the finish line.*

Sand Springs steals the Lake Placid.

Voodoo Dancer captures the Diana.

Silver Wagon instills Derby dreams during the Hopeful.

Zavata scores in the Amsterdam.

In one of the most impressive performances of the meet, Ten Most Wanted captured the coveted Travers, becoming the 134th winner in the race's storied history.

POST TIME
520
APPROXIMATE ODDS
1
2
3
4
5
6
7
8
9
10
11
12
13
14
15
16
All Betting & Cashing

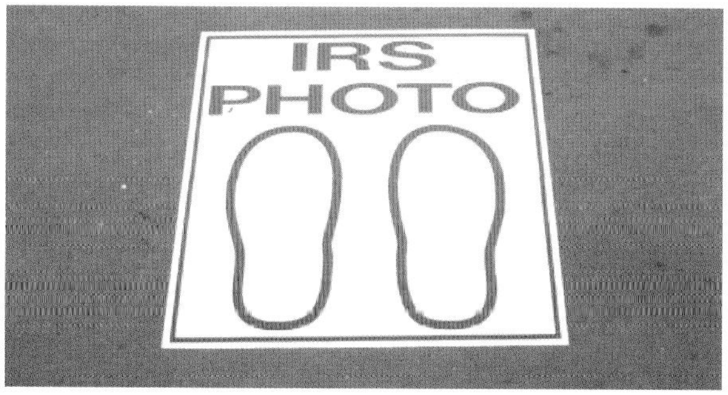

Winning at the races is easy: First you bet, then you cash—and if you're lucky, you'll pay a visit to the IRS teller.

What better way to celebrate a winning day than with a Funny Cide beer?

Saratoga's best,
awaiting the
start of the race.

CHAPTER FOUR

THE JOCKEYS

"A jockey is no mere passenger on a racehorse. His role in bringing home winners is critical and demanding. First, jockeys must have an exquisitely fine sense of pace over each furlong. . . . Positioning relative to the field is also critical."

—LAURA HILLENBRAND, *Seabiscuit*

TO BE THE BEST, you have to beat the best. And if you're a jockey, that means picking up your tack, hitting the New York Thruway, and settling in Saratoga for the six-week season that defines the best of the best in Thoroughbred racing.

Both praised and reviled for what they do—or don't do—on the back of a horse, jockeys live with the threat of death every day. The best riders are fearless yet calculating, imbued with both great strength and a delicate touch. It has been said that pound for pound, jockeys are the most talented athletes of any sport. After watching a day's worth of races, it's hard to disagree.

Throughout its illustrious history, Saratoga has witnessed tremendous feats by the top riders in the sport. For years, Saratoga was Angel Cordero's house. The Puerto Rican-born jockey, who now makes his living as John Velazquez's agent, won an incredible 13 riding titles in 14 years—including 11 in a row. "If a horse has four legs, and I'm riding it," Cordero once said, "I think I can win." Clearly, Cordero instilled that attitude in his protégé Velazquez, who had a season for the ages in 2003. Proving that his record-setting six-win day on Labor Day in 2001 was no fluke, Velazquez piloted a remarkable 61 winners, shattering the previous mark of 55 set in 2001 by Hall of Famer Jerry Bailey.

Imagine Derek Jeter walking through the bleachers at Yankee Stadium before taking the field. It would never happen. But Saratoga has always provided an intimate racing experience. After each race, the jockeys traipse through the clubhouse, past a sea of admiring and disgruntled bettors, as they make their way back to the jockeys' room to get ready for the next race.

Bailey, who won seven riding titles in eight years, is a Saratoga mainstay, as are other top jockeys, including Pat Day, the lifetime-earnings record holder, and Edgar Prado, 2002's leading rider.

In this chapter are images of these stalwart warriors—a band of brothers and sisters who devote their lives to the sport. There are portraits and poses; candid shots and action shots; victory celebrations and a dangerous spill. The expressions on the riders' faces say it all: *What we do isn't easy, but we wouldn't want it any other way.*

Shane Sellers (right), who captured the 2000 Travers on the big gelding Unshaded, and Edgar Prado, Saratoga's leading rider in 2002, take some time out of their busy day to hobnob with the fans.

Saratoga traditionally brings together many of the best jockeys from across the country. Normally based in Kentucky and Florida, respectively, Robby Albarado (top left) *and Cornelio Velasquez made Saratoga their summer home and mixed it up with the likes of New York regulars Mike Luzzi* (above), *Aaron Gryder* (bottom left), *and Jean-Luc Samyn.*

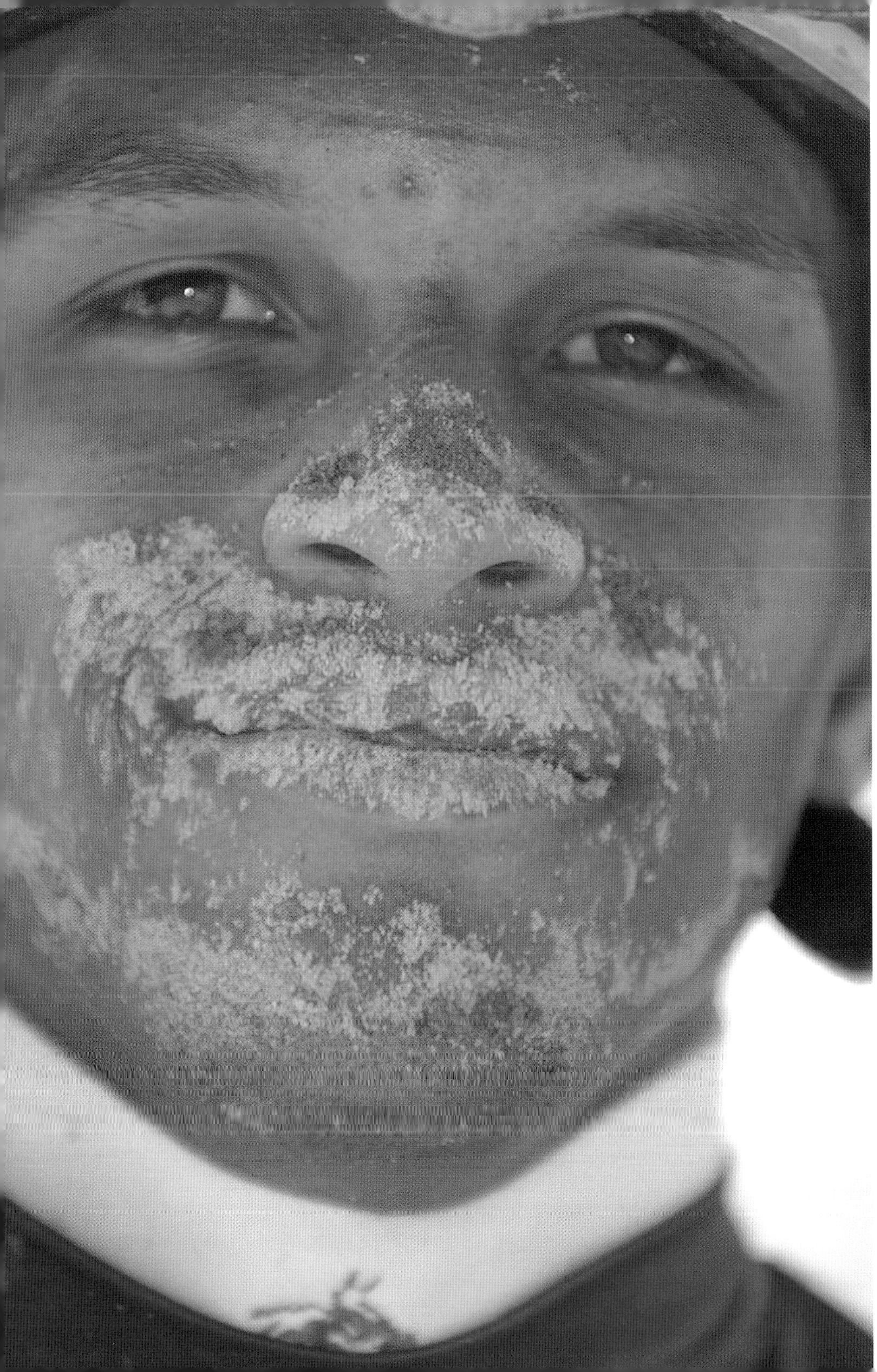

Dreams are often made and dashed at the Spa—and the meet hasn't always been kind to apprentice jockeys. In [illegible] *competing for six grueling weeks with the best in the sport. Fragoso finished with seven wins; Cotto came up empty.*

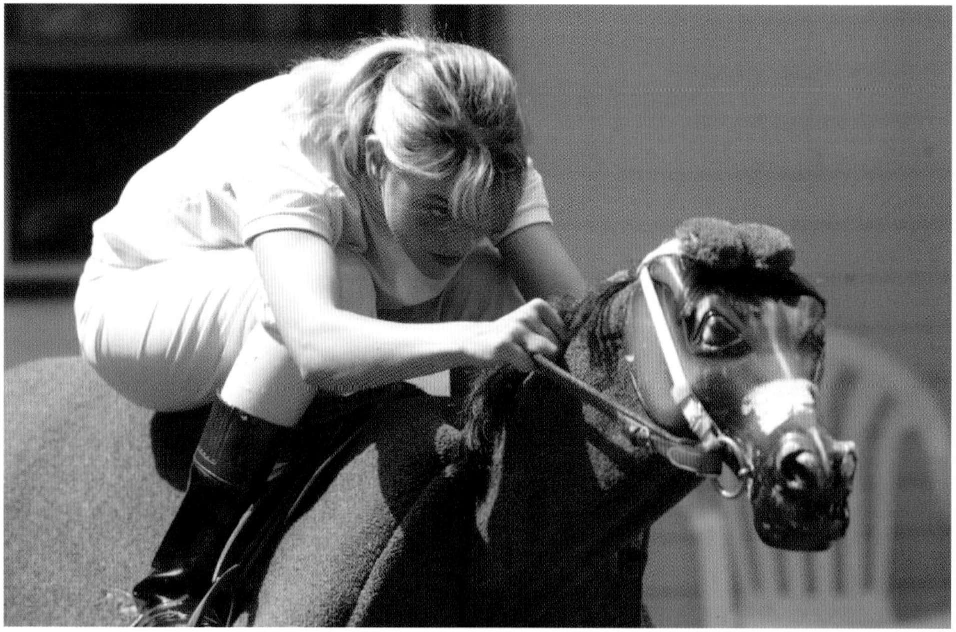

Three's company: jockey Shannon Uske, working the Equicizer, tries to follow in the footsteps of Hall of Famer Julie Krone, who tied a Spa record in 1993 (since broken) by winning five races in one day. Steeplechase jockeys Danielle Hodson (bottom right) *and Blair Waterman look to do the same, trying to emulate the great success of Blythe Miller, who dominated the jump races before her retirement in 2003.*

The dangerous lives of jockeys: Steeplechase jockey Danielle Hodson is tended to after a spill.

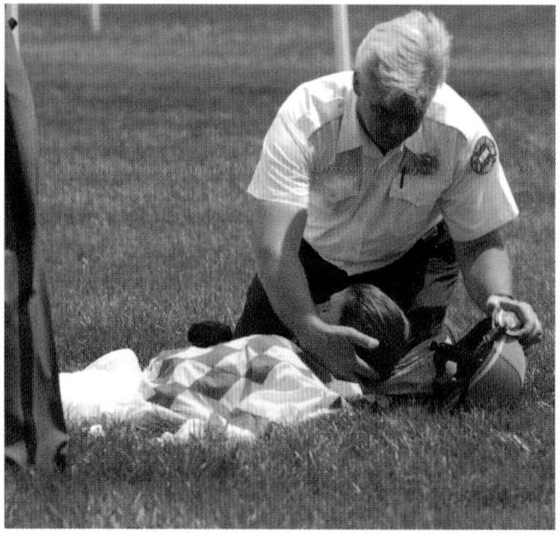

Thoroughbred horse races come in many shapes, with many subplots. Some are predictable, others as unforeseen as a sudden collision or as uncontrollable as a high-strung race-horse's moods. Good riders win the races that go according to well-laid plans. Great riders win the ones that defy logic and demand split-second adjustments and reactions.

—PETE AXTHELM, *The Kid*

The jockeys, in their neat, multicolored, incandescent silks, boots glistening in the sun, whip at the side, entered the walking ring, proudly—bullfighters disdainful of the crowd.

—JACK ENGELHARD,
The Horsemen

The eye in the sky looks down on Jose Santos, wearing the maroon-and-gray silks of Sackatoga Stable, as he talks with Funny Cide's trainer, Barclay Tagg, and assistant trainer Robin Smullen. Funny Cide didn't race during the meet, but his presence was felt everywhere.

Any ambitious American boy who stops growing and stops eating at the age of twelve can earn an income of from $10,000 to $250,000 a year before he's old enough to vote. He also has to learn to ride a horse, but that's the easy part.

—DAVID ALEXANDER,
A Sound of Horses

John Velazquez may have won the riding title in 2003, but Jerry Bailey, seven-time leading rider and one of the best ever to compete at Saratoga, always makes his presence felt.

Jorge Chavez, affectionately known as Chop Chop for his aggressive riding style and hand-pumping action, has enjoyed his share of success at the Spa, but perhaps his greatest triumph came on May 5, 2001, at Churchill Downs, when he guided Monarchos to Kentucky Derby victory.

Edgar Prado, 2002's leading rider, celebrates after one of his 39 wins at the 2003 meet.

"The Mig"—Richard Migliore—sitting chilly on Northern Rock, who finished fifth in the Whitney.

Two of the best—Jerry Bailey, on Empire Maker, and John Velazquez, on Strong Hope—duke it out in the stretch run of the Jim Dandy. Bailey's furious rally on Belmont Stakes winner Empire Maker came up just a nose short, thanks to the masterful ride of "Johnny V.", who squeezed every last ounce of energy out of his mount.

Shaun Bridgmohan strikes a pose in the hot August sun.

With purpose in his stride and a bounce in his step, John Velazquez heads off the track after a race.

Pat Day, at 48 years old, set the lifetime-earnings record when he surpassed Chris McCarron on August 10, 2002, after guiding With Anticipation to victory in the Sword Dancer Invitational. Day's biggest victory of the 2003 meet, however, came aboard the 3-year-old colt Ten Most Wanted, who won the Travers in dominating fashion.

Trainer Nick Zito talks strategy with jockey Eibar Coa.

CHAPTER FIVE

THE TRAINERS

"I came to think of trainers as Renaissance princes who ruled the backstretch. Walking the shedrows I saw that each barn resembled a principality, embodying a unique blend of laws and mores, an individuated style. Brightly colored placards bearing trainers' names or initials or devices shone in the sun, and it was possible to intuit the flesh of a prince from the sign he displayed."

—BILL BARICH, *Laughing in the Hills*

A THOROUGHBRED HORSE'S welfare begins and ends with the trainer. There are few animals on earth as fragile as a Thoroughbred—a thousand or so pounds of muscle and bone propped up on four spindly legs that look more appropriate for a ballet dancer than a half-ton animal that runs at nearly 40 miles per hour. With so much at stake, the care and feeding of such delicate creatures demands a never-ending watchfulness from the trainer, who runs his "principality" as he deems fit.

Each trainer's approach or style is different—some are born horsemen and can spot a problem with a simple laying on of the hands; some are brilliant managers or charming glad-handers who can rally the troops and keep a prying owner at bay; still others are experts at reading the condition books and masterfully spotting their horses. Yet one thing remains the same: No one knows the horses under his care more intimately than the trainer.

Seabiscuit would not have been Seabiscuit had trainer Tom Smith not been able to recognize the horse's peculiarities. Carl Hanford intuitively knew the whims and fancies of the great Kelso. Ben Jones, "Sunny Jim" Fitzsimmons, and Charlie Whittingham just plain understood horses. All good trainers know horses—they speak a language we mere mortals can never hope to understand.

In full cowboy regalia, Hall of Fame trainer D. Wayne Lukas—like a prince atop his steed—commands his charges on an August morning. Lukas has six Saratoga leading-trainer titles to his credit, and will go down as one of the greatest Triple Crown trainers in the history of the sport.

In his book *The Wrong Horse*, William Murray sums up this quality best, when writing about trainer Brian Mayberry and his family: "It takes a lifetime of being around horses to be able to succeed at the racetrack. I've stood beside the Mayberrys at the rail in the early morning hours, watching them supervise the workouts and outings for their animals, and they never misidentify one of them. Often Brian can't remember the name of the horse I ask him about, but he knows which one it is—'the gray one' or 'the bay filly' or 'that new two-year-old.' He knows and I don't, and that's the key to the whole relationship between the two categories of people, trainers and owners, who dominate the sport."

The images in this chapter include some of the more famous trainers in the sport—and some of the not so famous. They are the faces of men and women who've spent nearly every day of their lives looking horses in the eye and discerning whether they are fit to run that day. They are the faces of the old and the new, the legends and the up-and-comers. They are the faces of the princes of the sport.

Surrounded by a sea of media, Funny Cide's trainer, the normally reserved Barclay Tagg, plays a cat-and-mouse game with the press when asked about Funny Cide's preparation for the Travers. The Kentucky Derby and Preakness winner eventually skipped the "Midsummer Derby."

"TRAINER'S LAMENT"

I'm not allowed to train the horse,

The way that I know best.

I'm not allowed to pick the race,

My judgment fails his test.

I'm not allowed to choose the jock,

That he does with zest.

But if the damned horse runs bad,

My ignorance he'll attest!

—JOHN H. CLARK, *Trader Clark*

"The Giant Killer," Allen Jerkens, who sent out Onion to upset the mighty Secretariat in the 1973 Whitney, enjoyed another typical Saratoga season in 2003: This time his Puzzlement upset 2002 Breeders' Cup Classic winner Volponi in the Saratoga Breeders' Cup.

Patrick Biancone, a wizard with maturing 2-year-olds, starts the day with the sound of horses.

If you are to make your living around horses, it's important to have a discerning eye, as trainer Ken McPeek illustrates in this photo.

The old guard: P. G. Johnson (bottom left), *who trained 2002 Breeders' Cup Classic winner Volponi; LeRoy Jolley* (top left), *whose champion Foolish Pleasure won the Hopeful in 1974; and Scotty Schulhofer, whose Lemon Drop Kid captured the 1999 Travers.*

And the new guard: Christophe Clement (top right), *whose star filly Voodoo Dancer won the 65th running of the Diana; George Weaver* (bottom left), *a former Todd Pletcher assistant who proved he was ready for prime time; and Steve Asmussen, who, in 2002, was the nation's leading trainer by wins with 407, making him only the third trainer in racing history to reach the 400 mark.*

The backstretch . . . did have a lot in common with the circus . . . And training horses, like walking a tightrope or swallowing a sword, wasn't something you could go to school to learn; it was a trade passed on from person to person, along with a load of practical wisdom and a soupçon of balderdash.

—Carol Flake, *Tarnished Crown*

Regulars on the New York circuit: Rick Violette (opposite) *and Yankees fan John Parisella on horseback, and Richard Schosberg with his trusted friend.*

The husband-and-wife team of John and Donna Ward have had many successes at the Spa, but perhaps their most notable victory came in 2001, when they sent out Monarchos to win the Kentucky Derby.

Most trainers are born to the game by way of fathers, brothers, uncles, cousins, or family friends. Others enter through side doors. Former trash collectors, CIA agents, dance teachers, salami salesmen, professors, ski instructors, jockeys, policemen, pool sharks, car dealers, and caterers have all trained Thoroughbreds.

—JAY HOVDEY, *Inside Horse Racing*

Bobby Frankel enjoys some down time with his dog, Happy. Frankel has won his share of stakes races at Saratoga—including the 2003 Whitney with Medaglia d'Oro. Later in the year, the four-time Eclipse Award-winning trainer broke D. Wayne Lukas's single-season record for North American Grade 1 stakes wins.

The man with the tan from Florida, Ralph Ziadie, scored big during the 2003 meet when his 2-year-old colt Silver Wagon ran a big one in the Hopeful.

He may have had some trouble getting off this horse, but Todd Pletcher had no trouble saddling winners, which he did at a 28 percent clip, setting the record for most wins at a single Spa meet with 35.

Jonathan Sheppard can flat-out train over jumps and on the flat. One of his biggest feats was saddling With Anticipation to consecutive victories in the 2001 and 2002 Sword Dancer.

Though his big hoss, Mineshaft, didn't race at the Spa in 2003, Neil Howard still couldn't stay away.

"Professional trainers have the quick eyes of the faro dealer and the pressure-resistant nerve of the safecracker."

—Tom Ainslie,
Ainslie's Jockey Book

Though Todd Pletcher earned top trainer honors in 2003, that spot had previously been occupied by Hall of Fame trainer Bill Mott, who has eight leading-trainer titles under his belt.

Hall of Fame trainer Shug McGaughey, who has trained some of the sport's best for the Phipps racing dynasty, walks the shedrow, injured arm and all.

[illegible] — it's one of the only sports in which men and women compete on a level playing field. Female jockeys have succeeded at the highest levels, as have female trainers, including Linda Rice, whose barn is usually loaded for bear during the summer meet.

The legendary Seabiscuit, standing sentry outside the National Museum of Racing and Hall of Fame.

CHAPTER SIX

The Immortals

"The process of evolution never ceases, and this is as true of horse trading as of anything else. There always is something new to learn in the horse business, if you are observant. If you are not willing to learn and accept new ideas and new methods, you might as well lie down and let them put the flowers on your chest."

—Humphrey S. Finney, *Fair Exchange*

In 1968, Fasig-Tipton opened a new sales pavilion at Saratoga and christened it the Humphrey S. Finney Pavilion, named after the legendary horse trader who served as president and chairman of the Fasig-Tipton company. Each year, the Fasig-Tipton Saratoga Selected Yearlings sales attract thousands of owners—foreign dignitaries, software magnates, self-made men, and landed gentry—all trying to outbid each other in an attempt to land the next Seattle Slew. The sales also attract race fans and curiosity seekers who cram the pavilion, hoping to witness history as it unfolds. To say, two years later, that you saw the hammer drop on the winner of the Kentucky Derby when he was just a yearling is certainly worth boasting about.

And though it's hard to re-create the excitement of the sales, the Humphrey S. Finney Pavilion comes to life once again when the National Museum of Racing and Hall of Fame conducts its induction ceremony for that year's honorees. It's a fitting venue, because, in a way, the Humphrey S. Finney Pavilion is a place where legends are born and perpetuated.

Not too far from the pavilion, down Union Avenue and across from the track, those legends are immortalized at the National Museum of Racing and Hall of Fame, a treasure trove for racing fans eager to celebrate the horses, jockeys, and trainers who have transcended the sport.

On the next few pages, the sales and the induction ceremony come to life.

Banners about town alert the weekend horseplayer to the 2003 Affirmed exhibit, celebrating the life and career of the 1978 Triple Crown winner and two-time Horse of the Year.

Banners commemorating the 11 Triple Crown winners grace the front window of the museum.

*The National Museum of Racing and Hall of Fame
Thoroughbred racing's nirvana.*

RACING
MEMBERS OF
RACING HALL OF FAME

Recent inductees include 1985 Breeders' Cup Sprint winner Precisionist; Dance Smartly, the only filly to sweep Canada's Triple Crown; and the late Sonny Hine, trainer of 1998 Horse of the Year Skip Away. Accepting for Hine is his wife, Carolyn, who owned Skip Away.

Fasig-Tipton's Humphrey S. Finney Pavilion plays host to the Hall of Fame induction ceremony.

Past inductee Jerry Bailey presents 2003 inductee Mike Smith with his Hall of Fame plaque. Smith, a two-time Eclipse Award winner, won three straight leading rider titles at Saratoga, from 1991 through 1993, and now makes his living on the Southern California circuit.

"The players, some several dozen multimillionaires seated in choice locations, with another few hundred lower-bracketed participants distributed in the remaining seats and

Out back, the attendees enjoy the festivities.

The next Triple Crown hero?

"We who conduct the sales invade the field of histrionics, in our own not-completely-subtle way. We ham it up a little. We enjoy getting laughs and contriving to pit one buyer against another, and many of the attitudes and artifices of the sale are used to cajole the customers and keep them in a generous frame of mind."

—Humphrey S. Finney,
Fair Exchange

"The fashion show begins. Horses that have been brushed, groomed, polished and braided for the last week . . . are led out by grooms from their 8' x 10' stalls, in which they have been sequestered all night. This is one fashion show in which you can touch the merchandise . . .

Lips are curled back for looks at teeth; hocks are felt for heat; hooves are lifted in search for cracks. If a yearling bucks or rears, 'My! That's the Buckpasser in him! Should go for a pretty price . . .'

—Bernard Livingston,
Their Turf

The horses feel the electricity in the sales atmosphere, strutting around before potential buyers.

The bid spotters spot the action, signaling to the auctioneer that someone just upped the price.

Inside the ring, the horses are just as curious as their future owners.

A panoramic view from outside the pavilion—onlookers trying to catch a glimpse of the next million-dollar baby.

The 2003 Horse of the Year, Mineshaft, goofs off behind the scenes.

CHAPTER SEVEN

PORTRAITS

"Throughout the years of the Thoroughbred it has been the effect of horses on humans that has been the most remarkable aspect of racing. Eclipse made a gentleman out of an arrant rogue named O'Kelly. Old, old men will challenge you to a fist fight if you take the name of Man o' War in vain. A hard-bitten, cynical gambler who watched Equipoise, one of the gamest horses in history, drive home in the 1930 Pimlico Futurity after he had gone to his knees at the start, said, 'When you see a horse like that, you believe in God for a minute.' . . . No other animal has ever affected the emotional nature of man so much as the Thoroughbred race horse."

—DAVID ALEXANDER, *A Sound of Horses*

IF YOU WALK through the National Museum of Racing and Hall of Fame located on Union Avenue directly opposite the track, you're treated to a cornucopia of racing history. Images of the greatest race-horses, along with those of their owners, trainers, and jockeys, are enough to make even the hardened punter go soft. Then, to realize that many of these horses actually raced across the street is titillating. Saratoga, it seems, always manages to make history.

Some horses, such as Runaway Groom, Thunder Rumble, and Fourstardave, scored their greatest triumphs at the Spa; other truly great ones, including Man o' War, Gallant Fox, and Secretariat, suffered improbable defeats. Every year, a fresh group of horses—from downstate New York, Florida, Kentucky, California, and even as far away as Ireland and New Zealand—competes at the Spa

Funny Cide's bête noire, Empire Maker (who thwarted Funny Cide's Triple Crown bid in the Belmont Stakes), had a troubled Saratoga. Who knew that his gutsy second-place performance in the Jim Dandy would be his last?

and new heroes emerge and old records are broken. Some horses run the races of their lives, others stumble, and still others, like 2003's Horse of the Year, Mineshaft, are just there to relax and rejuvenate. After all, what creature wouldn't enjoy spending six weeks at Saratoga?

The legendary newspaperman Joe H. Palmer once wrote a column entitled "Saratoga, or the Horse at Home." The images that follow are portraits of horses at rest and at play—but, for six weeks of the year at Saratoga, most certainly at home.

Funny Cide didn't race at the Spa in 2003 but had a busy summer nonetheless. The media hounded the gelding and his connections so much that something as inconsequential as a sneeze warranted a mention in the papers.

Peace Rules put in yet another impressive performance in what turned out to be a very impressive 3-year-old campaign when he finished second to Ten Most Wanted in the Travers.

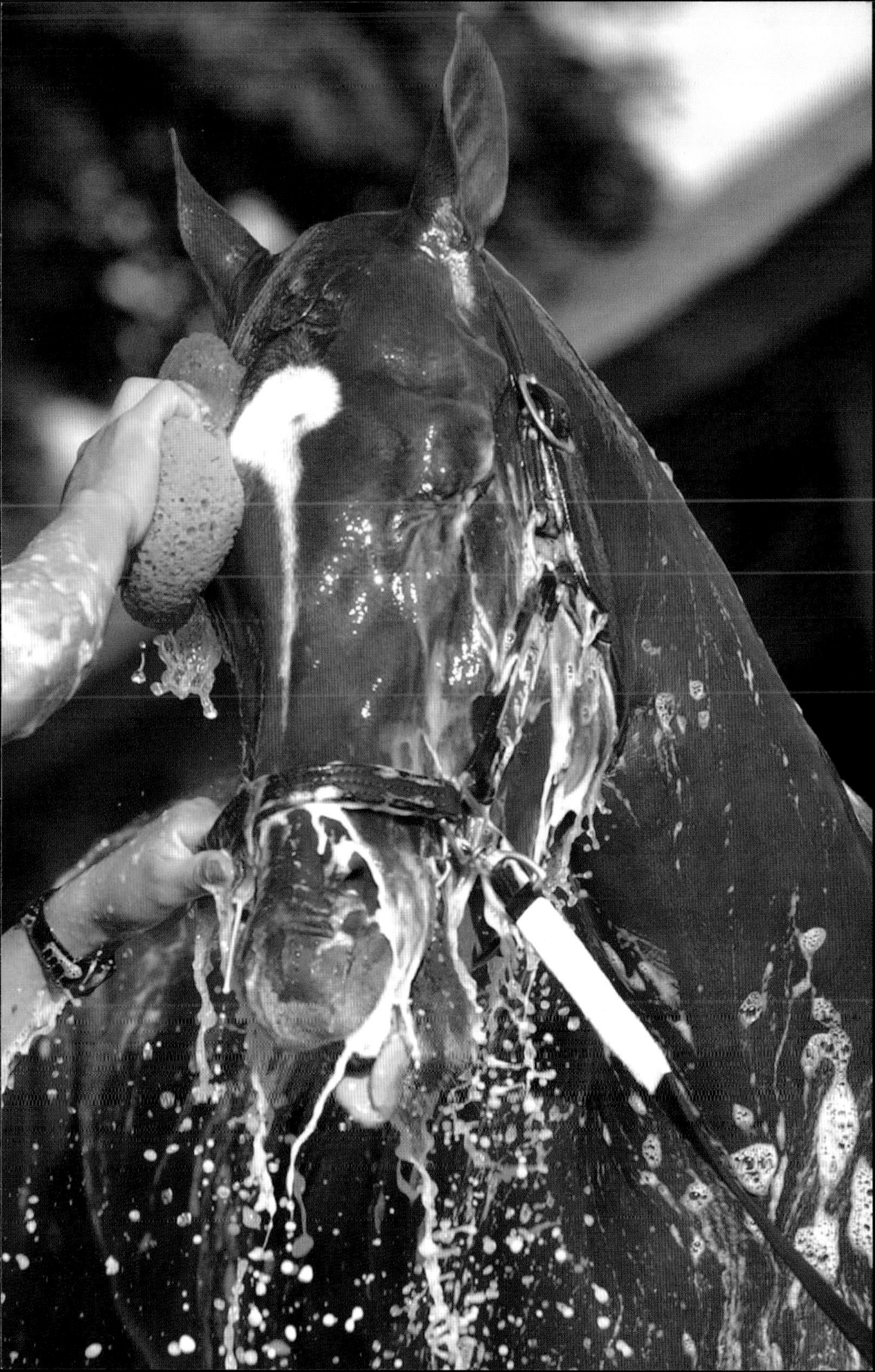

The Steve Asmussen-trained Lady Tak gets the royal treatment. Her big Saratoga win came in the Test.

Volponi, the 2002 Breeders' Cup Classic winner, came to Saratoga to ready himself for a title defense. He left with second-place finishes in the Whitney and the Saratoga Breeders' Cup.

Value Plus was apparently pleased with his maiden victory on July 26 and his second-place finish in the Saratoga Special.

"There is something about the outside of a horse that is good for the inside of a man."

—Sir Winston Churchill

". . . what the horse supplies to man is something deep and profound in his emotional nature and need. It will endure and survive until man's own nature changes."

—William Faulkner,
"Kentucky: May: Saturday"

With Anticipation

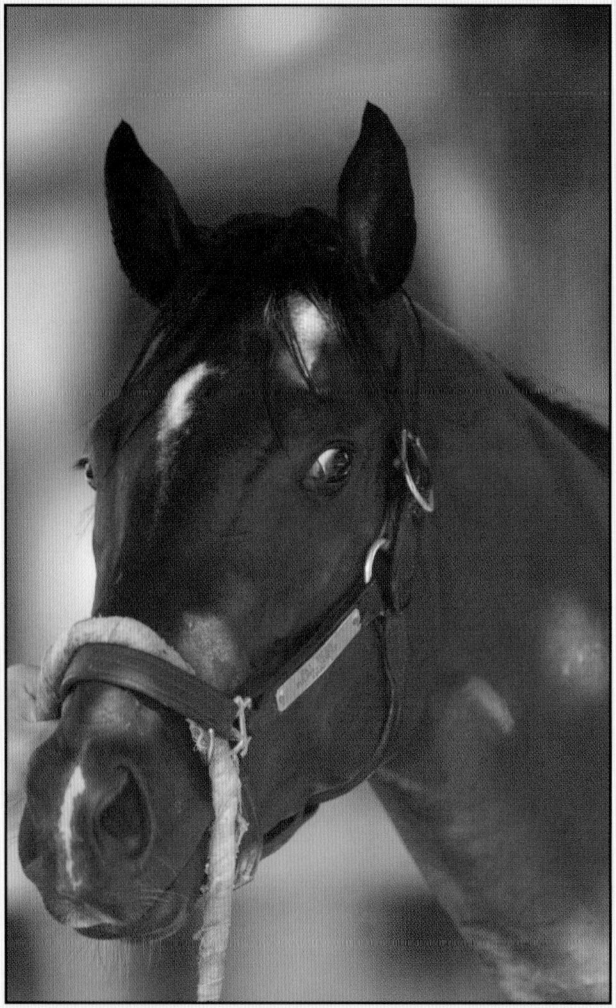

The talented but injury-plagued Sky Mesa, who finished a disappointing last in the Travers.

The marvelous filly Voodoo Dancer, who won the Diana.

Travers winner Ten Most Wanted.

A pair of terrific Bobby Frankel-trained fillies: Sightseek and Heat Haze.

Fewer sights are more rewarding to weary travelers than this sign welcoming them to Saratoga Springs.

CHAPTER EIGHT

THE TOWN

"One of the finest things that ever has happened to mankind is Saratoga. The pleasant summers and bubbling springs have been appreciated by residents and visitors for more than two centuries . . . Saratoga is something special. I hope it remains forever a part of the great Thoroughbred sport. I think it will, because it means so much to so many people."

—HUMPHREY S. FINNEY, *Fair Exchange*

BEFORE THERE WAS ever a town or a racetrack, there were the springs of Saraghoga, as the Native Americans called it; hence Saratoga's official name, Saratoga Springs—the place of swift water. In 1802, a pioneer by the name of Gideon Putnam built a tavern for weary travelers not too far from Columbian and Congress Springs and the rest, it is said, is history. Build it and they will come—and they most certainly did. Because of the medicinal properties of its springs, Saratoga became a bustling resort town, and because of its appeal as such, big spenders from all over the East Coast made it their summer home.

Naturally, where there's money, there's bound to be gambling. So on August 3, 1863, the first race meet was held. Soon after, gambling halls started cropping up, the most famous of which was Canfield's Club House, run by Richard Canfield. High rollers such as "Diamond Jim" Brady, John "Bet a Million" Gates, and Arnold Rothstein became Spa regulars, as did the Broadway set of Lillian Russell, Fanny Brice, and Peggy Hopkins. Saratoga wasn't only the August place to be—it was the place to be *and* be seen.

"Like any fashionable destination, Saratoga has had its ups and downs, but it has always been a place with mythic restorative powers. Before one came to Saratoga for the horses, one came for the waters, for the saline springs that bubble up from layers of limestone and shale through the cracks of the Saratoga Fault."

—Carol Flake, *Tarnished Crown*

Saratoga has long been known for its curative mineral springs, which helped make the town a tourist attraction more than two centuries ago. The Columbian Spring, discovered in 1803, is located in Congress Park (though it no longer flows with mineral water).

Time stands still at the Spa: At the east end of Congress Park, where Circular meets Union, this impressive flower bed alerts tourists to what day it is.

In addition to its various springs, Congress Park, a quiet little sanctuary that sits off Broadway, houses the Carousel and the legendary Canfield "Casino," which serves as the annual site of the Whitney Ball.

But the rollicking gambling heyday couldn't last forever. And when the glitz and glamour and decadence of the resort town were finally tempered by reformers, all of the fads of the times disappeared, but two things remained: the town, with its quaint charm, and the racetrack, where gambling was still legal.

There is an old adage: The more that things change, the more they stay the same. Truer words could not be spoken of Saratoga. Yes, the town has changed drastically over the last 200 years. But in a way, it hasn't changed at all, as the images in this chapter illustrate. Broadway still runs through town, the springs still flow, and the racetrack—that dowager queen of the American turf—sits like a red-and-white Taj Mahal, awaiting its yearly worshippers. And boy do they come—not just for the track, but for everything this charming rustic town, nestled in the foothills of the Adirondacks, has to offer.

A look down Broadway, the main thoroughfare in a town that revolves around Thoroughbreds.

"In July and August, there's nothing like it in the whole country. Races every day, gambling, millionaires and pickpockets and sporting people and respectable family folks and politicians and famous theater actors and actresses. You'll find them all in Saratoga."

—Edna Ferber, *Saratoga Trunk*

Some familiar sights on Broadway: the Adirondack clock, so that serious players don't miss post time; the famed Adelphi Hotel, a rare surviving High Victorian Hotel Inn from 1877; and the Saratoga Army & Navy store.

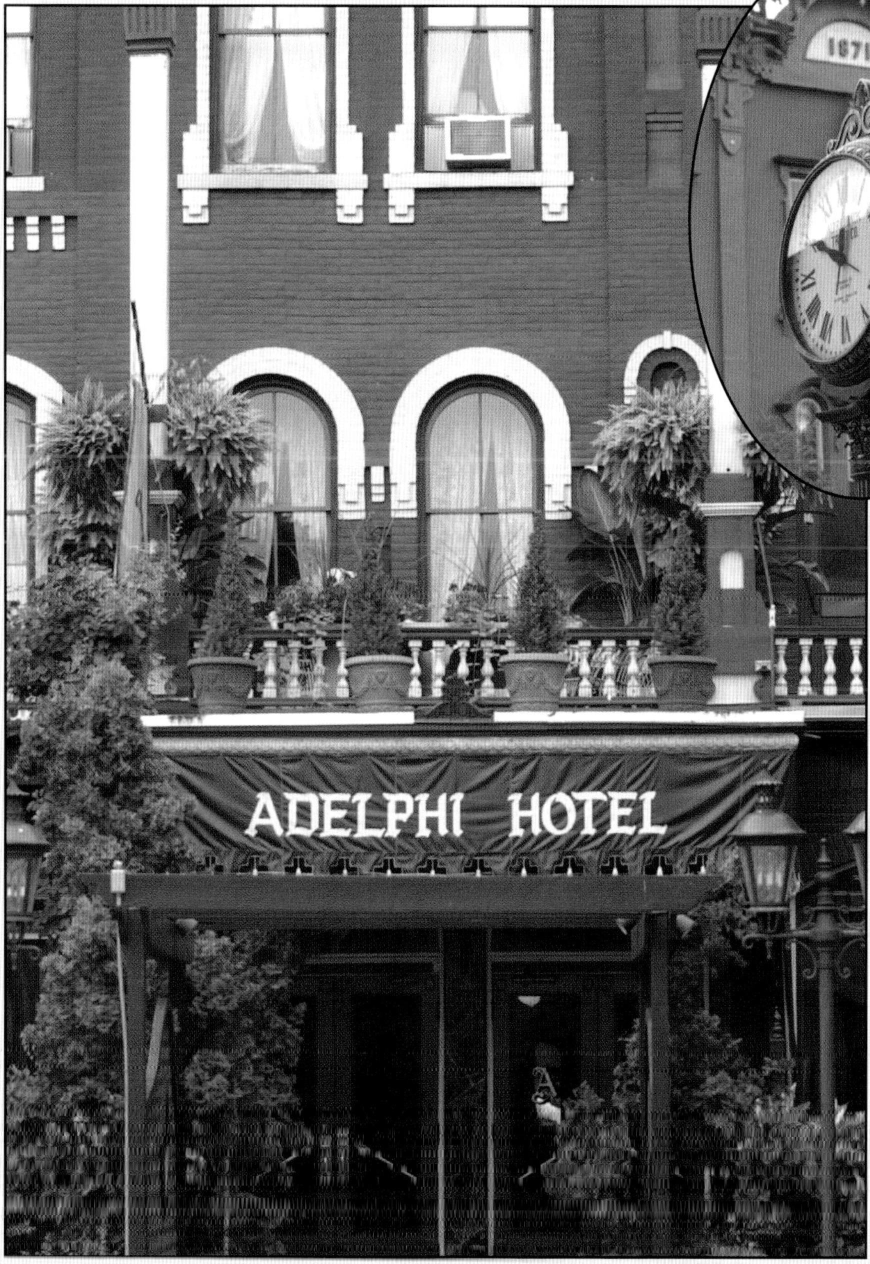

The horses aren't only at the racetrack. Equine art adorns Broadway, and a horse-drawn carriage cuts through a majestic August night.

> They came to ride, to drive, to dress, and to secure that freedom from business and domestic care that gives perfect rest and brings back bodily health and vigor.
>
> —NELLIE BLY in the *New York World*

Saratoga represents more than a vicarious triumph. It is a successful turning back of the pages, a stroll through the mirror, the slow drop of Alice down the rabbit-hole. It is a month of living in about 1910, though some visitors insist that the hotels take this too literally. And I suppose that in the year Novelty beat Iron Mask for the Hopeful Stakes, a dollar would have gone further, though from what I hear it went as fast.

—Joe H. Palmer,
"Saratoga, or the Horse at Home"

Victorian mansions dot the landscape of the town.

The famous Siro's dining establishment—the Saratoga place to be—where owners, trainers, and players go to celebrate or drown their sorrows after another day at the races.

At 20 Lake Avenue sits the home office of The Saratogian, *the town's newspaper since 1855.*

The Funny Cide store, located at 40 Caroline Street, was a testament to the popularity of the New York-bred gelding and his upstate owners.

It's not easy to escape the hustle and bustle of the town and the track, but just a stone's throw away is Yaddo, the renowned artists' retreat created by Spencer and Katrina Trask. Here, famous writers—among them John Cheever, Truman Capote, and Sylvia Plath—as well as painters, musicians, and photographers, have honed their craft.

The Avenue of the Pines leads into the Saratoga Spa State Park, a National Historic Landmark, which is also home to the Hall of Springs, the Lincoln mineral baths, the Saratoga Performing Arts Center (SPAC), and the Gideon Putnam Hotel.

"Prancing and snorting on the edges of our consciousness, like vestiges of a myth, certain horses seem to suggest a means of venturing out into the world and conquering it. And racehorses, with their inordinate will to win, represent the ultimate symbol of worldly longing. With racehorses, whether you own them, watch them, or bet on them, you seem to be reverting to some older, darker way of looking at the world, a way of testing your fate, of finding your place in the scheme of things."

—Carol Flake, *Tarnished Crown*